Football

GAME

INTELLIGENCE

The Difference-Maker in Officiating

By Jeffrey Stern

FROM *REFEREE* MAGAZINE & THE NATIONAL ASSOCIATION OF SPORTS OFFICIALS

Football Game Intelligence: The Difference-Maker in Officiating

By Jeffrey Stern, senior editor, Referee/NASO

Cover and layout by Matt Bowen, graphic designer, *Referee* magazine

Published by Referee Enterprises, Inc., and the National Association of Sports Officials.

Printed in the United States of America

ISBN-13: 978-1-58208-160-1

TABLE OF CONTENTS

INTRODUCTION

There has been a sea change in the officiating industry over the past 20 or so years. No longer does an official's job begin with the opening whistle and end when the clock hits all zeroes at the end of the fourth quarter. The responsibilities, expectations and scrutiny for officials have led to changes in rules, procedures and policies.

The successful official (certainly the wise one) accepts those changes and adapts to them. The only way to stay on top of things is to improve one's game intelligence. That's what this book aims to do.

Between the covers of this book you will find chapters that deal with such matters as pregame preparation, dispatching one's duties in a thoughtful, even-handed manner, postgame reflection and the legal ramifications of officiating. That last one is more important than ever before and is one that cannot be overlooked.

A number of skilled writers and talented officials contributed to this book. They are Jon Bible, a former NCAA Division I and NFL official who now works in the United Football League; George Demetriou, veteran high school and small college official; Alan Goldberger, the nation's leading expert on law relating to sports officials; Jerry Grunska, longtime *Referee* contributor and former official; retired NCAA Division I official Judson Howard; and Tim Sloan, veteran official and frequent *Referee* contributor. I also wrote some of the material.

I hope you find the book lively, useful and informative. Here's hoping it takes your game intelligence to new heights.

Jeffrey Stern
Senior editor
Referee magazine

CHAPTER

01

RISKY BUSINESS

Abraham Lincoln was once asked to describe what it was like to be President of the United States during the Civil War. Lincoln's answer cited the story of a man who was tarred and feathered, then ridden out of town on a rail. When asked how he liked the experience, the man replied, "If it weren't for the honor of the thing, I'd rather have walked."

Sometimes it seems that making calls with the goal of giving both teams an equal chance to win, is the "honor of the thing" for all officials. To be sure, the specter of accountability that looms over every call or no-call that we make as officials goes with the territory.

Referees have been sued for many things: For calling fouls and for not calling fouls. For ejecting a fighting player from a game and for not ejecting a fighting player from a game. For starting a game in inclement weather and for not starting a game. For providing first aid and for not providing first aid. The list goes on and on. In short, officials have been sued for about anything they do or don't do in the course of a single game.

Officials, in the eyes of players, coaches and team followers, sometimes make decisions that affect the outcome of games. As you know, officials often make a decision on the field even when they make no call. Football officials are, to be sure, decision-makers. Decision-makers are sometimes held accountable for their decisions when those decisions are perceived to be in error. That accountability sometimes takes the form of a lawsuit.

WHAT MAKES AN OFFICIAL LIABLE?

When an official takes the field, the law generally holds the referee to a standard: He or she must work the game as would a "reasonably prudent referee." In some states, legislatures have lowered the official's standard of care by making officials liable only for so-called "gross negligence," or "reckless disregard" of safety principles. Generally, though, to avoid legal liability an official's actions should reflect reasonable efforts to safeguard players and others from injury. That means officials need to be ready, willing and able to manage risk by enforcing the rules.

Successful officials avoid "liability hotspots" by demonstrating the following attributes:

Rules knowledge. A thorough understanding of the rules is required if players, coaches and onlookers are to be protected from bodily injury.

Mechanics. Competent officials manage risk by being in the right place and using approved techniques to enforce all rules dealing with safety-related issues.

Courage. Prudent officials do not permit anyone to prevent them from tending to the tasks at hand.

The appearance of impartiality. We all know officials are impartial. Officials don't care who wins the game. But do you exhibit the appearance of being impartial? Successful officials know the difference between perception and reality and act accordingly.

What are the areas of officiating that tend to put officials to the test? Experience tells us that certain aspects of officiating present legal liability landmines that need to be addressed. Consider the following seven hotspots of officials' liability. The areas were selected because they generally apply to all officials, and to some degree at all levels of play. They are listed not by "weight" but in the chronological order encountered by officials in the course of an assignment.

FACILITIES

- "We've been playing here for six years and you're the first official who said anything. Give the kids a break."
- "The county just spent $2 million redoing this field. The other team just traveled 75 miles. And you won't let us play.

Who are you kidding?"
- "Those chains have been used all season. No referee has ever said anything. You guys need to get together!"
- "I've got 800 people in the stands. The cops are on overtime. We're gonna play this game. I'll take responsibility."

Who among us has not heard remarks such as those when trying to have a dangerous facilities condition corrected?

Officials are required by most rules codes to inspect the field. Unsafe conditions are found in some very unlikely places. From the architects to superintendents to business administrators to building principals to athletic directors to site managers, unsafe and nonconforming facilities continue to be hatched.

Whatever the reason, someone decided not to look at the applicable safety rules regarding materials, clearances, buffer zones and hazardous design defects. When the great equalizer referee arrives at the field, his or her blessing is all that is needed to start the action! Should a participant or onlooker be injured due to an unsafe facility, the chorus will sing out: "The referees thought it was OK or they wouldn't have started the game."

Whatever the reason for the existence of an unsafe facility, an official cannot always avoid that liability concern. Clearly, some facilities are unsafe by design and cannot be corrected in the few minutes before the game. Those conditions should be reported, in writing, to your commissioner or association. However, many other physical hazards can be neutralized by padding, buffering or simply removing or relocating the hazard. If the condition can be remedied before the game by physically removing the unsafe item from the playing surface, padding or buffering, you need to direct that the corrective action be taken before the game starts. If management refuses to make the adjustment, do not play the game. Simply stated, if protecting an area, such as a vault pit or drain plate, will make the area reasonably safe, it is no excuse that game management does not have any padding on site. If their response is to say they don't have any padding or can't find it and an injury occurs, they will blame you for starting the game in unsafe conditions. Do not fall into that trap.

EQUIPMENT

Like facilities, equipment issues require the official to have a detailed knowledge of the rulebook and a good sense of what equipment will unreasonably increase the risk of injury.

Although rules codes at different levels contain different restrictions as to what type of equipment, clothing and ornaments are "legal," meeting rulebook requirements for *legality* is not quite the same as legal in the sense that you will not lose a lawsuit.

Rulebook requirements for legal equipment are the best and only starting point for determining what type of equipment and accessories to allow participants to use. But for prudent officials, more is required. Questions need to flash up when there is any doubt as to player equipment, clothing or accouterments: Is the item, technically legal by rule, worn or affixed in such a way that it presents a danger to the wearer or another person? Is the item properly fitted? Is the item worn or affixed in the manner intended by the manufacturer? Does the item bear the certifying stamp (NOCSAE or other) required?

Administrators, coaches and supervisors are required to have appropriate equipment and uniforms on hand. If they do not, it is not your fault. Indeed, some rules codes, including NFHS rules, require the head coach to verify to the referee that his or her team will wear and use legal equipment during the game. If equipment and/or uniforms are illegal by rule, in disrepair or ill fitting, safety may be compromised.

Officials are the last line of defense in those situations. It is indefensible for an official to permit any athlete — on any level — to participate with unsafe equipment or accessories. Officials who disregard player safety in that respect will find that seriously injured players or spectators will be quick to point the finger of blame in the form of a lawsuit.

GAME CONTROL

When do we "let them play" and when do we take the game away from the players? The answer to that question eludes many referees, but it's at the heart of managing risk. Most times when a fight or serious injury occurs, some keen-witted observer is heard to say, "The officials let the game get out of control." That statement is, of course, usually preceded by a game in which the players decided they did not want to play but rather to commit unintelligent fouls, taunt opponents and look for alibis.

Under those circumstances, competent officiating always will take the game away from the players, as they say. The alternative, in terms of legal liability, is unacceptable. Indeed, some rules codes, including all NFHS rules, require the head coach to verify to the referee that his or her team will exhibit good sportsmanship throughout the game.

Liability can sometimes be measured by three simple equations: Bad officiating encourages anti-social behavior. Anti-social behavior equals injuries. Injuries equal lawsuits.

There are tools available to deter the type of behavior that can spell legal liability. The negative consequences that flow from a rule violation are a major deterrent to conduct, which leads to injuries. Officials must make every effort to prevent injuries — both intentional or otherwise — by penalizing uncivilized conduct and illegal contact infractions.

Officials must penalize immediately the cheap shot, the taunting and baiting, the finger in the face, the attempts to humiliate an opponent or the trash talk. The plain facts are that all of the above activities can lead to violence. Violence leads to injuries. Injuries lead to lawsuits.

We have all heard officials warn players: "The next time you do that it's a foul." Unfortunately, the next time may be the cause of an injury that spells liability, especially since you have already told the people involved that you saw it happen the first time or second, third or fourth and you didn't do anything about it.

As to fighting, an ounce of prevention is worth 100 pounds of cure. How do officials prevent the fight? The answer is simple: Prevent the fight with good mechanics. By the negative reinforcement of penalizing uncivilized actions, officials prevent it by making sure that all players must be under observation by somebody at all times and reacting swiftly and firmly to unduly aggressive behavior exhibited by players.

Officials who are alert to sense ill-will brewing and let the opponents see that striped shirt in between them when something starts to happen. That includes, of course, not having everybody's back turned on the players ever — no matter what else is going on in the game or elsewhere.

INJURY MECHANICS

Without a doubt, the other side of game control is what to do in the event that you can't prevent an injury. In the event that a participant is injured, managing risk includes utilizing proper injury mechanics. The following steps must be taken:

- Determine if the player really is in need of assistance. If so, beckon the coach or athletic trainer at the first opportunity.
- Don't attempt to treat the player yourself.
- Don't discuss the cause of the injury with anyone.
- Don't request anyone to move the injured player so that you can get the game started again. It does not matter if the

delay is one minute or four hours. Only the medical personnel, once you've called out the coach, can and should determine if the player can be moved and when.

- Keep opposing players on the field separated.
- Continue to supervise both teams, including bench areas.
- Remember rules specific to players exhibiting concussion-like symptoms.
- A player who is bleeding must be treated before resuming participation.

WITHER THE WEATHER?

If your mother ever told you to come in out of the rain, she may not have been wrong. From an official's standpoint, once a game begins, the dangers created by inclement weather are almost totally under the officials' control. Why? Simply because most rulebooks leave any decision to suspend play due to weather or environmental conditions up to the officials — and no one else.

For that reason, officials may bear the primary legal responsibility for injuries to participants that are caused by weather conditions. Not only the obvious meteorological phenomena such as lightning, but the effect of torrential rain and the like on the condition of the field or equipment has been cited in lawsuits brought against officials.

If there is any doubt that weather will create an unreasonable risk of injury, err on the side of caution and suspend play. Don't wait to "finish the last two minutes." Do it immediately. Be aware that severe weather events are for you as the official to recognize and deal with. Coaches and administrators will inevitably attempt to distance themselves from any responsibility for weather-related injuries in a lawsuit by claiming that the officials were in charge and they (the coaches/administrators) had no say in calling the game off.

Unusually high winds blow things around. Torrential

rain can impact a playing surface beyond what athletes can or should be reasonably expected to endure. Lightning can strike too fast to avoid it any time its presence is detected by sight or sound. Any environmental condition that creates enhanced risk needs to be evaluated by officials before the injury occurs — not after.

SPECTATOR INTERACTION

Officiating manuals uniformly caution officials against talking to or reacting to the comments of spectators. That is good advice to avoid that liability concern. When an official engages in dialogue or debate with a spectator, the conversation can place the official at legal risk — as well as at risk for injury. What's more, to elevate a spectator to the status of your inquisitor is indefensible, legally speaking. Remember: There are no qualifications to attend a sporting event. Spectators who taunt officials are rewarded when the official makes them "important" by talking back. Good officials do not elevate the status of spectators.

If a spectator is disrupting your game, the correct and risk-wise mechanic is to direct the site manager (or head coach if there is no site manager or security personnel) to remove the spectator. No part of that mechanic involves the official addressing the spectator directly.

Some years ago, a high school referee requested the removal of the father of one of the players. As luck would have it, the spectator-father happened to be a school board member and the referee happened to talk to the press after the game.

The referee was reported to have told a newspaper reporter that the parent of the player got his attention by exhibiting "lewd and aggressive" behavior "when his behavior crossed over the guidelines of sportsmanship."

When the father/spectator/school board member

threatened to sue the referee, the official wrote a letter apologizing.

The state high school athletic association said that it didn't believe that the school board member's comments were lewd. Then it said that it thinks it's important that people understand that officials are not perfect and referees make mistakes, but it sincerely believed they were doing the best job they could on that specific evening. That's right, nary a word spoken by the state association about what the school board member/parent did, inciting a crowd with unsporting behavior at his son's game. Instead of taking the school board member/parent to task for creating a dangerous situation by his remarks, the state association is apologizing for the official.

Similarly, offhand remarks or discussions about game officials' work when somebody gets hurt — or about game officials' work when a team member got hurt — can lead to legal consequences.

DISQUALIFICATION CHALLENGES

With the advent of the summary suspension rules in both high school and college rules and regulations, referees face legal challenges of a different sort. In those cases, physical injuries are not the focus of taking an official to task in court. Rather, the object of the plaintiff is to have a judge engage in "further review" for the purpose of reversing the official's call assessing a flagrant or disqualifying foul or infraction.

Since most disqualification rules and regulations do not provide for any appeal of an official's decision to show the door to a violating player or coach; and since that decision involves in many cases an automatic suspension for the next game or two, legal complications sometimes develop after ejections.

The significance of such disqualifications increases when penalties are immediate (i.e. suspension for the next game or two, etc.). Cumulative disqualifications (i.e. successive or repeat violations during the same season) may increase the length of the suspension.

As penalties increase, so does the likelihood of litigation. Officials need to be extra vigilant to follow approved mechanics in disqualification situations. Offhand remarks concerning the details of a suspension, threatening players or coaches with suspension and failing to utilize approved mechanics can make defending a disqualifying foul difficult.

Officials are paid for their judgment. They are bound to conduct the game as the rulemakers intend it to be played: fair play in a safe environment for those participating. The starting point in practical terms can be seen by reviewing the areas where officials have definite responsibilities, spelled out in black and white. Those areas represent the bare minimum in terms of an official's duty. At the end of the day, rules knowledge, mechanics and courage will go a long way toward avoiding liability — and make you a better official.

AN OFFICIAL'S LIABILITY CHECKLIST

You can't prepare for everything, but the following list can help you avoid liability concerns.

Before the Game

☐ Perform all pregame responsibilities.
☐ Identify site manager or person in charge of venue.
☐ Avoid careless discussion of teams or personalities.
☐ Review weather and field conditions with crews.
☐ Be on the field when your jurisdiction begins.
☐ Maintain the appearance of impartiality.

Facilities
☐Inspect the field/court and surroundings for hazards.
☐Check padding and clearances.
☐Instruct assistant officials.

Equipment
☐Is the equipment illegal by rule, or just plain unsafe?
☐Look for projecting hard substance.
☐Don't allow jewelry if rules prohibit it.
☐Check the fit and appropriateness of uniforms.
☐Keep doctor's permission slips in your permanent file.

Game Control
☐Always keep a set of eyes on athletes and benches.
☐When an infraction occurs, penalize; don't "warn."
☐Penalize taunting and baiting without hesitation.
☐Penalize unsporting and other illegal contact by rule.
☐Don't permit players to fight.
☐Remain aware of trouble spots (pile-ups, sidelines, etc.).
☐Don't threaten participants with impending suspension.
☐Don't engage in discussion concerning prior actions of a
    player or coach involved in an ejection.
☐Don't discuss the consequences of a disqualification.
☐Don't render interpretations of a suspension/
    disqualification rule.
☐Don't police suspensions in subsequent games.
☐Deal with disruptive spectators by deploying site
    manager/security. Don't address spectators directly.

Injury Mechanics
☐Determine if player needs help.
☐Don't render first aid or move a player. Let medical/team
    personnel attend to the player.
☐Don't talk about the cause.
☐Separate the teams, but maintain sight lines.

☐ Communicate with crew as to rules specific to injuries.

☐ Follow blood/communicable disease indicator rules.

Postgame Mechanics

☐ Follow specific end-of-game procedures.

☐ Locate crews and leave together.

☐ Don't seek out coaches or engage in conversations.

☐ Don't stay on the field after the game officially ends.

☐ Lock dressing room door.

☐ Don't give media interviews. Discuss the game only with assigner, association member or commissioner.

☐ Prepare game reports stating only facts.

General

☐ Consider the welfare of players your first responsibility.

☐ Enforce all safety rules, regardless of the level.

☐ Don't discuss skills or abilities of athletes and coaches.

☐ Have a plan for emergency situations.

☐ Understand game control: "Don't turn your back."

CHAPTER

02

YOU'VE GOT NEXT

One of the stickiest situations that officials can face is entering a game with a coach who has publicly proclaimed that he got hosed by another crew or a particular official the week before. The coach knows going in that you've likely heard about the incident, and he will think that, in the fraternity spirit, you or your crew will show support for the other by giving him a triple dose of what he thinks he got the week before.

The coach will also think that you're thinking that he is thinking evil and paranoid thoughts about you, and that you'll react to his first question or comment by declaring war. You may in fact be thinking some or all of the above, so that at the drop of a hat you'll think he is unfairly taking out last week's frustrations on you.

How to deal with that scenario in which you are, at best, wary of each other and walking on eggshells and, at worst, almost in open combat from the get-go? There's no perfect solution, but there are some ways to make the best of what has the potential to be a bad situation.

WHEN LAST WEEK'S CREW WAS INVOLVED

When the coach is mad at someone else, you have two main working premises, and everything you say or do is ultimately geared toward them. First, you don't want history lessons before or during games you work; that is, you don't want to hear about who did what last week or, for that matter, several plays ago. The old adage "each day is a new day" should be applied and you should expect coaches, players, administrators and others to take the same position.

The second premise is to make it clear you will not listen to coaches talk badly about fellow officials. To do so is unethical, unprofessional and just plain wrong. The problem, of course, is that sometimes the folks on the other side are not singing from the same song sheet. It soon becomes apparent that they are going to say something before the game come hell or high water, and/or take their frustrations out on you during the game by making sundry accusations about our motives in calling the game as you are.

Your first task is to take care of the officials working with you that day. Then worry about coaches. Although you need to remember you're dealing with adults, you will not ignore the elephant in the room by saying nothing. Instead make it clear in your meeting with the coach that what went on before is old news and that you must approach this game as you would any other, with the same intensity, focus and professionalism that you try to exhibit in every game. Stress that you cannot react any differently to things that the coach might do or say than you normally would — in other words, you can't react more quickly or harshly. But by the same token you can't cut them any extra slack.

When another crew or official is involved, you need to be even more adamant about not having a history class than you would be if the coach was mad at you. Too many officials try to pacify coaches and curry favor by listening to them gripe about how horrible so-and-so was — or worse, agreeing with them. Don't be one of those.

If the coach wants to bring up last week's incident, say something like, "Coach, with all due respect, that didn't involve anyone working this game. Let's focus on today, and we'll give you the best job we can."

There's no list of magic words to use, because every situation is unique. But by trying to be polite, stressing the positive aspects of steering clear of last week and focusing on today, you have a better chance of success. Steer clear of that kind of criticism, no matter what you have to do or say to get the conversation redirected.

If the coach insists on pushing the issue, you have to get firm. Even if that means the coach gets mad at you and perhaps, down the road, doesn't want to use you again. If that happens, so be it. There will always be other places you can work. Respected

COMMUNICATING WITH COACHES — THE RIGHT WAY

Not all communication between coaches and officials is negative or confrontational. There are plenty of opportunities to converse with a coach in a professional way before, during and after a game. Sometimes you can even — gasp! — share a chuckle with a coach. In moderation, of course.

Here are some tips for dealing with coaches in a positive way.

• Communicating a problem. If a player is becoming mouthy to officials or opponents but not to the point at which a penalty is called for, let the coach know about it. Players will often push the envelope because they're testing the officials' limits of patience. But because coaches have the biggest carrot for athletes — playing time — a player is more amenable to an attitude adjustment when it's suggested by a coach. Also, most coaches would rather discipline the player than suffer whatever consequence may arise from a penalty or ejection for the player.

• Sharing information. Officials often receive warnings of approaching inclement weather. Letting the coaches know of a potential stoppage in advance can prevent a situation in which a coach feels taken by surprise. Adjustments allowed by rule — such as reducing playing time — can be agreed upon by both sides without rancor.

• Answering questions. It's not uncommon for coaches to move from the high school to college ranks or vice versa. As a result, they might not be acquainted with rules at the level they're now working. If a coach asks a question in a professional manner during a stoppage or before or after the game, answer it. Although officials delve into rule changes, coaches are often less diligent about examining them. If a new rule is particularly technical, the coach may ask you to explain the nuances. Let the coach know you're glad to be asked, then explain the rule using the simplest terms possible. Giving examples of situations in which the rule might come into play is also helpful.

• Shooting the breeze. Between plays or quarters, coaches might initiate a causal conversation. It's OK to participate as long as it's a chat and not a discourse, and it's as unobtrusive as possible. The topic is important as well. Beware the coach who asks, "Have you officiated any (fill in name of conference rival) games yet?" You're not a scouting service; your job is not to offer opinions or information on other teams or players.

When your dressing room is the coach's office, the coach or assistants invariably have to come in to retrieve something or other. If their visit is brief and doesn't turn into an attempt to curry your favor, accept it as part of the vagaries of working amateur ball. If not, politely ask the coach to leave so that the officials can finish dressing and get on with their pregame.

officials take a red-line before they'll pacify a coach by listening to him vent about what other officials did on another day.

The bottom line is: Business as usual. Realize that's sometimes easier said than done, but if you can't set your mind to take that approach, maybe you don't belong in the business.

IF THE COACH DOESN'T BROACH THE TOPIC

There will be occasions when the coach will say nothing about the previous event. In those cases it's best to let a sleeping dog lie, even if the coach's body language tells you that he is seething. Some might argue that raising the issue can be a good, clear-the-air preemptive strike. That's an option, but to bring up a coach's public airing out of last week's crew or official when the coach hasn't done so is guaranteed to produce harm. Besides, what can you really say? "Coach, I know you're ticked off over what happened last week, but please remember it wasn't us"? There aren't a lot of words or tones of voice calculated to yield a positive result. At the very least, that approach sends the message that the topic is at the forefront of your mind, and while it may be, you will derive no benefit from the coach knowing that. At worst, it sounds like groveling. In sum, if the coach leaves it alone, so should you.

IF THE COACH BRINGS UP LAST WEEK TODAY

References during the game to the previous event should not be tolerated. Comments such as, "Are you guys trying to screw me worse than I was screwed last week?" are attacks on your integrity. Let the coach know, in no uncertain terms, that you're not going to travel down that road. Don't "pile on" a coach by getting after him after another official has done so. That's usually counterproductive. But do it if you think it's an unusual circumstance that warrants the repeat.

Although you don't want to cause a big stir, you cannot allow yourself or your crew be the victims of such attacks. You might not throw a flag or resort to an ejection the first comment out of the chute. But by communicating as positively and professionally as possible, you will get the message across and the comments may well stop.

The same holds true if the opposing coach implies you are trying to "even things up" for the aggrieved coach by favoring that team. Common comments include, "Are you trying to kiss his rear after last week?" During an opportune time, sidle over and say something like, "Coach, I'm sure you like to think of yourself as a professional. So do we. We don't do business that way."

If that doesn't work, you've no choice but to get firmer. The bottom line is you cannot tolerate such behavior.

WHEN YOU WERE THE OBJECT OF THE COACH'S WRATH

How do you handle a situation in which the coach went ballistic the last time you or your crew had his team? Your reaction might depend on whether or not you blew the call.

If you find out that you made a mistake the last time you worked that coach's game, give him a chance to vent during the pregame meeting you have with the coach. That should be done as long as it's a private affair involving the concerned parties and there is no carryover to the field. Go in to that meeting thinking that he should be allowed that venting. If it happens before the game and you get it over with, you might be able to move on and have a good game.

Give the coach a chance to get rid of the venom. When the coach broaches the topic, you can say, "You're absolutely right. You got it stuck straight up your backside that day. Now, I could give you a lot of excuses about what happened and what's been done to fix it, but you don't want that.

You've been waiting for two weeks to rip me apart, so go for it. Say whatever you want — no holds barred."

There will probably be some other back-and-forth, but the windup is that the acknowledgment will likely disarm him and defuse things. You can at least start the game with a clean slate. And don't be shocked if the coach doesn't take you up on your invitation to let loose.

If you think you didn't screw up, try to head him off with something that seems to suit the mood, such as "Coach, I think everyone will be better off if we don't go down that road. That game is over and done with and we need to focus on today."

The exact words will depend on the situation. But in the end you want to, as tactfully as possible, get the coach to turn the page. No good can come from a, "You guys screwed up!" "Oh, no, we didn't!" exchange that may escalate into a shouting match. Even if it doesn't, such a debate is unlikely to be productive. If necessary, you can remind the coach that if he feels that strongly, there are channels through which to register that discontent.

THE END GAME

Assigners and supervisor continually, and properly, stress the need for officials to be approachable, communicative, non-confrontational and the like. But in the end, those attitudes must take a back seat when it comes to impromptu history lessons from coaches. While you will do everything possible to tactfully redirect conversations that are going down the wrong path, standing firm in the face of attacks on your integrity is a must.

CHAPTER

03

LIVEN UP YOUR PREGAME

It has been said many times that a sound pregame conference is a vital part of working a good football game. But what's the difference between an effective pregame and a waste of time?

A pregame has three functions: continuity, preparation and motivation.

A referee must get the officials on the same page in terms of how they will work together. The pregame is not the time to review the mechanics of each position. On the contrary, assume everyone knows who will bring the captains out for the toss, where to be on kicks, etc. Instead, focus on how our positions intersect. On a sweep, when will the wingmen turn the pitchman over to the referee? How will they work the play if the offense has trips to one side and some or all crisscross after the snap?

If the crew stays intact during the season, and especially if it has been together for several years, you don't need to dwell on the basics every week. Better to do a thorough review before the first game, to clean out the cobwebs that have accumulated since the last season. Thereafter, focus on a hodgepodge of topics like fumbles or goalline plays. If possible, cover 10 or so different situations each week, using a variety of methods described later. Bottom line: Pregames should be productive but also fresh.

It is important for the referee to prepare the crew for the teams playing that day. Avoid going into a game with firm notions of what each team will do (such as run the option, throw screen passes) because teams often don't stick with the script. Moreover, if you are on top of our individual and crew mechanics, you should be prepared for whatever happens.

On the other hand, it doesn't hurt to remind yourselves that team A has a punter who can kick 70 yards, that team B runs a no-huddle offense or that one of the quarterbacks is especially adept at faking a handoff. It also helps to know that one team tends to be mouthy if there has been bad blood between the teams in the past.

Finally, the referee should get the crew in a positive frame of mind. Crews work better if they are loose and in good spirits, and the pregame is where either the right or wrong mood is set. A crew can't afford to be lulled into a sense of complacency because it had a good game the previous week, just as the crew can't be in a bad humor because it made mistakes. While talking about what went wrong last week, the crew should also discuss what it did right. In fact, stress always leaving the pregame on a positive note.

A pregame should not be a referee monologue; that makes people doze off and creates the perception of referee as dictator. Instead, everyone should participate. Time is also important, for the mind can only absorb so much. Most referees believe an hour and a half is about right, although there are times when only a few minutes can be had. That's usually the case for sub-varsity games, when people are getting off work at the last second. Finally, don't waste time on plays that may happen once in your career. Instead, focus on the bread-and-butter stuff you know will occur.

To make pregames innovative and fun, try variations in approach. Here are some that have been used to great effect.

Retired Big 12 referee John Laurie used a fold-up field with a green felt surface, field markings and poker chips for players and officials. He would lay it on a table and construct scenarios — bombs, fade routes, snaps over the punter's head, plays on the offensive and defensive five yardline — and move the chips accordingly. Each crew member would move his chip to show how he would work that play. For people who learn better with visuals than with words, that is ideal.

During the season, the referee can assign each crew member to run a pregame. One enterprising official scattered 30-40 index cards on a table. They were labeled "Criteria for catch," "Post-scrimmage kick enforcement," "Fourth-down fumble," "Defensive pass interference criteria," "Goalline coverage," etc. The officials went around the table choosing a card until they were gone, with each person having to discuss whatever pops up. Each person should choose three or four times in an hour and a half; the number can be adjusted based on the number of officials on the crew. That is better than assigning topics to people beforehand, because everyone must be ready to discuss anything on the spot.

Another official borrowed from the TV show *Jeopardy*. The crew walked into the meeting room to find six columns of cards taped to a wall, with the headings "Punts," "Kicks," "Passes," "Runs," "Line of scrimmage" and "Miscellaneous." Each column had six cards, marked $200, $400, etc.; there were even two "Daily Doubles." The crew went around the room with each person choosing a card; on the back were statements like "Fumble out of bounds rules," "Coin toss winner's options in overtime," and "Intentional grounding." Whoever chose had 20 seconds to cover all of the bases in the form of a question. If he didn't complete the answer in the allotted time, the next person tried and so on. When all of the cards were chosen, whoever had the most money was declared the winner, and the others agreed to buy him a postgame drink.

There are certain things that you need to cover in pregames to work well individually and as a team, but there is no reason that you can't do that in a creative and fun way. Try some of those pregame formats and you'll bring more enjoyment to the process.

CHAPTER

04

GET TIMERS, CHAIN CREWS ON YOUR SIDE

Time was winding down in a two-point game. A completed pass had given the offense a first down near midfield and raised hopes that a potential game-winning field goal could be in the offing.

Despite the officials' obvious signals, time continued to roll off the clock. The coach of the offensive team screamed at the officials.

"Seven seconds!" he declared. "I want seven seconds put back on the clock!"

The wing official assured the coach the officials were aware of the problem and would have the clock corrected.

"That clock operator screws us every time," the coach raged. "Who hires those people anyway?"

The wing official did his best to suppress a smile. "Coach, you're the home team. The home team supplies the timer." Needless to say, that ended the conversation.

In a high school playoff game a few years ago, the teams lined up for an anticipated punt. Suddenly one of the players on the receiving team started screaming, "Fake! Fake! It's a fake!"

The kicking team requested a timeout and the head coach fumed. He told the linesman that a member of the chain crew — provided by the home team and allegedly the father of one of the players — overheard the coach call for the fake and relayed the information to the nearest player.

Not out of out the realm of possibility but extremely difficult to prove.

Incompetent or unscrupulous auxiliary personnel like timers and chain crew members frustrate everyone. You will run across one or two every year or so. Your chances of having a good experience with timers and chain crews improve if you conduct a thorough meeting with them before the game. Here are some points to be covered in the meetings.

TIMERS

- **Is the timer experienced?** Some timers "have been doing it for 20 years" and don't feel they need instruction. Even if a timer insists he is capable, tell him it never hurts to review procedures. If the timer is inexperienced, you'll have to go through a more detailed run-through.

- **Is the clock operating properly?** Perhaps the clock malfunctioned last week or during the previous night's JV game. If so, ask the timer if the problem has been addressed. Either way, knowing there have been issues can cause the officials to pay special attention to the clock during the game.

- **How should the officials communicate with the timer if the clock needs to be reset?** That's easy if the referee is equipped with a microphone. If the coaches in the press box use headphones to communicate with the sideline, ask the sideline coaches to relay information. A last resort is to flash fingers to the timer in the same way a basketball referee reports a foul.

- **How long is halftime?** NFHS rules allow an extended halftime for special circumstances such as parents' night or homecoming. If the timer doesn't know or is unsure, the officials should find out from a representative of the home team how much time will be allotted for the intermission and relay that information to the timer. In NFHS games, when the clock for the halftime period expires, the timer should immediately put three minutes on the clock and start it. The three minutes must expire; the clock should not be stopped and reset for the third quarter even if the teams are ready to go before the three minutes expires.

Other reminders for the clock operator:

- **An official will act as auxiliary timer if the clock fails.** If the field clock becomes inoperative and is subsequently repaired, it will not be used again until the next period or when the referee determines it is operational.

The public-address announcer will indicate the field clock will not be official until the malfunction is corrected and a subsequent announcement is made on the public-address system.

• **Be alert for signals to start and stop the clock.** Any official may signal a timeout; therefore, the timer should be alert to stop the clock. On plays near the sideline and in advance of the line to gain, an official may give a winding signal to indicate the ball is inbounds and follow it by a stop-the-clock signal for an apparent first down. Remind the timer to be alert for both signals.

• **"Automatic" clock stoppers.** The clock should be stopped following a touchdown, field goal, touchback, safety or incompletion when the covering official gives one of those signals.

• **When to restart the clock.** After the clock has been stopped, it starts again on the referee's signal and if no such signal is given, the timer will start the clock on the snap without the signal from the referee.

• **The clock takes priority.** The timer should stop or start the clock before changing unofficial scoreboard information such as the down, distance and yards to go.

• **The clock doesn't run on trys.** Also, if an accepted penalty results in an untimed down at the end of a period, the clock should not be reset until the period officially ends.

• **Review running clock rules.** In games that use a running clock when a specific point differential is reached, be sure the timer knows the alternate rules.

CHAIN CREWS

Chain crews are like computers: They're taken for granted until they break down. That leads to a lot of confusion and frustration.

But when the officials (particularly the linesman) and the chain crew are well prepared and understand the others' role, the result is harmony worthy of a barbershop quartet. Here are some tips the linesman and chain crew can use to ensure a smooth performance.

Game management is required to make available a competent chain crew. It is strongly suggested the chain crew wear distinctive vests or jackets so they are easily recognizable. Ideally, only adults will be used for the chain crew. The chain crew is generally stationed approximately two yards off the sideline opposite the press box, except in stadiums where the total playing enclosure does not permit. If there is no press box, the location will be specified by game management at the request of the linesman. Unofficial auxiliary line to gain and boxes may be used on the sideline opposite the official line-to-gain and boxes. Those should also be approximately two yards off the sideline, except in stadiums where the total playing enclosure does not permit. The line judge is responsible for working with the auxiliary chain crew.

The best-case scenario is a four-person chain crew: Two to operate the chains, one to handle the box and one assigned to operate the clip. If the chain crew consists of only three members, the box holder can perform most of the clip duties while the trail line to gain holder tends to the box.

Before the game, the officials shall check the chains for accuracy. Ensure that the midpoint of the chain is marked with tape. That way you can readily discern if a five-yard defensive penalty will result in a first down. Remember that the rods at each end of the chain and the box must have flat lower ends covered by protective caps.

A pregame meeting involving the linesman and chain crew is absolutely essential. The linesman should find out the names of the chain crew (writing them down on your game card is a good backup), and then call them by name throughout the game.

As with the timer, it is not uncommon for a chain crew to want to skip the meeting. In those cases, the linesman should neither cave in nor become defensive. A good retort is, "That's great. I'm glad they didn't stick me with a bunch of rookies. But if you don't mind, there are a few reminders I'd like to provide just to make sure we're on the same page tonight."

As illustrated in the earlier example, because chain crews often consist of fans or even parents of home-team players, they must be reminded that they have forfeited their right to cheer or assist the home team in any way. They must think of themselves as an extension of the officiating crew. That means they must not interact with players, coaches, other team personnel or fans; must not comment about plays called by the officials; discuss strategy or argue among themselves.

The chain crew should be reminded that, if players approach, they must retreat and take the equipment with them. That protects the players and the chain crew.

The box holder is to take all spots from the forward point of the ball. In order to ensure accuracy, the linesman should go to the sideline and mark the spot with the heel of his forward foot after every play. It is important that the box holder doesn't change the down or move the box until the linesman communicates that information. In goal-to-go situations, the linesman can provide the box holder a beanbag. The bag can be dropped immediately behind the box and preserves the previous spot should the box holder have to move to avoid players.

Most chain crews understand they should not move the chains unless directed by the linesman, but the reminder needs to be offered. When a first down is declared, the trail pole goes immediately behind the box. The two must be lined up. The box should go in front of the chain rod so it is visible to the officials. The lead holder on the chain is responsible to ensure the chain is taut at all times. Once a first down is awarded to team A inside team B's 10 yardline, the chains are no longer needed and should be moved well away from the sideline.

The linesman's clip is a safety valve. If the chains are moved either in error or for safety reasons, the clip provides the exact chain location. The clip operator is to place the clip on the back edge of the line on the five yardline nearer the trail stake. The clip is never removed until the stakes are in a new position.

When the first or third quarter ends on a play that results in a first down, some crews set the chains and the clip before they switch ends of the field. It ensures that the chains are set correctly for the next period.

CHAPTER

05

MAKING HEADS OR TAILS OF THE COIN TOSS

Funny how something as simple as a coin toss can sometimes cause so many problems. Back in 1998, NFL referee Phil Luckett went with the first utterance from Pittsburgh captain Jerome Bettis, who started to say heads before switching to tails. It came up tails, the Steelers lost the flip and Luckett was forever branded by announcers and sportswriters as "the guy who screwed up the coin toss." Never mind that Luckett did the right thing according to NFL rules and that, despite Bettis' protests, enhanced audio revealed that Bettis had, indeed, changed his mind mid-toss.

Few fans, even true diehards, likely remember that a controversial flip decision almost cost one team the 1962 American Football League championship. The Dallas Texans and Houston Oilers played to a 17-17 tie in regulation, sending the game to overtime. Dallas won the flip. Abner Haynes, star running back and captain for the Texans, had been instructed to choose to defend the end of the field that would allow his team to take advantage of a gusty wind. But Haynes told the referee, "We'll kick to the clock."

As in the Bettis-Luckett case, the referee was obligated to go with the first part of that response. Haynes lucked out, however; the teams played one scoreless overtime period before the Texans won on a field goal 2:54 into the second overtime.

Celebrities selected to toss the coin of caused their share of problems for referees. Hollywood legend Liz Taylor was at midfield for the coin flip of a 1989 Redskins-Cowboys game in Dallas. Referee Pat Haggerty allowed Taylor to call the coin toss, and the movie star called heads. Haggerty signaled Dallas had won the toss. But the Redskins' captains protested, saying the visiting team is supposed to call the toss. The toss was conducted a second time. On the re-do, the Redskins called heads and won the toss.

Apparently Haggerty was a little star-struck. According to the Washington Examiner, Redskin captain Reggie Branch said, "She's a beautiful young lady. I think she hypnotized the ref."

The coin itself is an issue in some cases. Before Super Bowl XVII, former NFL referee Jerry Markbreit had trouble discerning which side of a ceremonial coin was heads and which was tails. A similar situation befell retired NCAA Division I official Dick Honig before the 2001 national championship game. In both cases, the referees had practiced the previous day with a conventional coin; the special coins weren't given to them until game day.

Late in the 2005 season, Mike Carey was the referee for a game between Detroit and Green Bay that was tied after regulation. As the camera zoomed in on Carey to capture the coin toss for overtime, viewers saw a panic-stricken Carey digging in his pockets for a coin. But the Californian's hand was so cold he couldn't extract the coin from his pocket.

Referees differ when it comes to what happens after they flip the coin. The NFHS manual says the referee is to catch the coin, but some referees — either not confident enough in their ability to catch or by choice — prefer to let it hit the ground. The CCA book, by the way, is silent on the issue. A local referee says he was a "let it hit" guy until one muddy night when the coin hit the turf and stuck in the ground on its edge. He reflipped it and, to his frustration and amazement, the coin landed the same way a second time.

Another referee had a habit of turning the coin over after he caught it. One day another official questioned him about that habit. "I've been doing it that way as long as I can remember. I swear I read it in the manual at some point in my career." Alas, a check of the manuals back to 1972 gives no such instruction.

Sometimes outside forces cause the problem. Consider this situation from several years ago, when five-official crews were not the norm. The start of a varsity game was

FLIP TIPS

The pregame meeting with the coaches is the official's first opportunity is to set a positive tone for the game, but the coin toss is the first visible and formal chance to make everyone comfortable that the game will be fairly administered.

The meeting of the captains is not a forum for prolonged commentary. Virtually nothing said will be relayed to other players and by the time the ball is kicked off, the captains will have forgotten whatever wisdom was announced. Anything you say can be misconstrued or misinterpreted and the coach will probably take offense.

There is no requirement or expectation to say anything at the coin toss other than what is necessary to conduct the business at hand. If the referee feels he has to say something, it's OK to remind captains that they are in charge of their teams and that officials may approach them on occasion for help. That may help solidify the status of captains as responsible individuals; however, it is not essential that be said.

The following should be avoided: reviews of past games, mention of rivalries, rules discussions, "helpful" hints and warnings. Starting the game with any form of warning or admonishment is setting the wrong tone and is inappropriate. The second-half meeting of the captains is an equally poor choice for such a discussion. If there were problems in the first half, they should be discussed directly with the coaches. A coin toss that lasts more than a minute after the captains arrive at midfield means the ceremony has gone on too long.

The preferred methodology is to have the captain make his choice before the coin is flipped. The choice should be repeated by the referee or umpire so that everyone is in agreement as to what was said.

Whether the referee catches the coin (with or without flipping it over) or lets it fall to the ground is one of the few remaining discretionary items. The drawback on announcing the coin will be caught is that a re-flip will be necessary if it is dropped. Allowing the coin to land runs the risk of having it roll away.

Offer the winning captain: "Defer," "receive" or "defend a goal," in that order. The order is that of the most likely selection and omits "kick." Kick is a valid choice, but one that, most likely, will get the captain in trouble. The officials may catch the overflow. If the captain was told to pick "kick," he will pick it, regardless of whether it is offered. There is no need to give him an opportunity to go astray.

If the choice is to defer, the declination should be signaled immediately. That will avoid unnecessary movement and posturing later on. The remaining choices are then presented and the captains positioned accordingly. If the choice is to kick or receive, only the first selection needs to be signaled. Once every few years, the choice will be to defend a goal. In that case, two signals are given. The first is pointing both arms towards the goalline being defended. The second is the appropriate signal for the other captain, probably to receive.

delayed because one of the officials in the four-man crew was involved in an auto accident on the way to the stadium. That fact didn't become known until the toss had already been conducted. A game in the same conference was being worked in a stadium several miles away by a five-man crew. A phone call from one game manager to the other led to the fifth man being taken off his game and dispatched to the game that was short one official. The trip took roughly 20 minutes.

Just as the replacement official took the field, the coach of the team that had lost the toss and chosen to defend the north goal approached the referee. "The wind shifted since we did the toss," the coach said. "I want to defend the south goal now."

"I'm sorry, we can't do that. The results of the coin toss are final," the referee replied. The coach argued that since the delay was not of his doing, he should be given the courtesy of a do-over. The referee stuck to his guns, however. Throughout the game the coach complained bitterly about every call — even those that went in his team's favor — and he berated the crew as it left the field after the game.

Many high school and youth football officials face ethical dilemmas at least once a season, it seems. You know the drill: A team wins the toss. When asked whether he'd like to kick, receive, defer or choose a goal, the flummoxed captain opts to kick or chooses a goal.

Some referees attempt to avoid what they know is going to be a problem by giving the captain a second chance ("You sure that's what you want? That means you'll be kicking off both halves") or flat out correcting the captain.

As a result, some referees adopt procedures to head off problems before they arise. Leaving out kick or defend as options works for some. Others ask the captain, "Do you want to receive before the first half or the second half?"

One white hat says that when he speaks to the head coaches before the game, he asks for the coach's preference if his team wins the toss. If one coach says receive and the other defer, he doesn't bother to toss a coin at all; he simply asks the captain of the team whose coach chose to defer which goal his team wants to defend. If both coaches say receive or defend, he flips as normal.

Any of the above methods will offend officials who follow Luckett's lead and take the captain at his word. They may do so with some discomfort ("I know it isn't right, but he said it"), but they forge ahead. It's difficult to argue with the hard-liners since they have the rulebook on their side. You can never go wrong by applying the letter of the law because it's absolutely defensible.

But even some sticklers will argue that the level of the game is crucial in their decision. While they would never allow the captains of a youth league team to make the wrong choice, captains of a high school varsity squad mess up at their own peril.

Understand, too, that trying to be helpful has its own risks. As the captains and officials gathered for the second-half choices of a JV game, the referee turned to the home team's captain. "It's your choice. You want the ball, right?" the official asked. "No, we want to kick," the captain replied. The referee said, "No you don't. You want the ball." The captain shrugged his shoulders and said, "OK, we want the ball."

When the referee signaled the choices, the home team's coach went ballistic. "I said we'd kick!" he screamed at the captain. The player related what happened at the meeting and the coach turned his wrath to the referee. Turns out the team's abysmal play on defense in the first half led the coach to decide his defense needed the work. Given the circumstances, the referee gave the coach his wish. The opposing coach was only too happy to get the ball.

Lest you think the answer to the falderal is to cut out the middle man — have the officials deal directly with the coaches and forgo captains — consider this incident that occurred several years ago.

Before the game the home team's coach told the referee, "We want to kick off because we're going to start the game with an onside kick. No matter what my captain tells you, we want to kick off." The referee expressed discomfort at being told to potentially ignore the captain, but he agreed and went on his way.

Sure enough, the stars aligned, the visitors won the toss and the visiting captain said, "We'll defer." The referee turned to the home captain. "And you want to ...." "Kick," the captain said, finishing the sentence and causing the referee to sigh with relief.

The onside kick failed miserably, the visitors took advantage of the short field to score a touchdown and used that momentum to build a sizable lead in the first half.

After the second-half choices were determined, the home coach stormed up to the referee, red-faced and obviously agitated. "What the hell did you do to me?" the coach spluttered. "I'm kicking both halves!" The referee reminded the coach of his pregame instructions.

"I only wanted to kick off the first half!" he said. "I want the ball in the second half. That's the rule!"

Which proves something, although only heaven knows what. Maybe it's that dealing only with the coaches regarding the toss isn't utopia after all.

CHAPTER

06

TAME THE TEMPER TIGER

Coaches can survive onfield temper tantrums; officials usually cannot. That is clearly an area in which there is a double standard.

We all know what anger is, and we've all experienced it. Anger is a completely normal, usually healthy, human emotion. But on the field, it almost always leads to problems.

Anger is "an emotional state that varies in intensity from mild irritation to intense fury and rage," according to Charles Spielberger, Ph.D, a psychologist who specializes in the study of anger. Like other emotions, it is accompanied by physiological and biological changes. When you get angry, your heart rate and blood pressure go up, as do the levels of your energy hormones and adrenaline.

According to Robert W. Westermeyer, Ph.D, research has shown that angry people show changes in their thinking. Typically people become "single minded," focusing exclusively on what they believe is provoking them. Needless to say, prolonged anger will affect judgment.

Anger is typically activated when a person believes he has been deliberately provoked. The instinctive, natural way to express anger is to respond aggressively. To a coach, the threat is losing the game, because of the perception that the officials are making mistakes. Anger inspires powerful, often aggressive, feelings and behaviors, so in the coach's mind, he is merely defending himself.

To the official, the threat is the coach's behavior. The natural response for an official is to lash back at anything or anyone that is irritating or annoying, but officiating protocol and common sense place limits on how far retaliatory anger be taken. Getting angry is not going to fix anything; it won't make the official feel better and may actually make him feel worse.

Logic defeats anger because anger, even when it's justified, can quickly become irrational. Cold, hard logic should be used. Take the approach that no one is "out to get you." You're just a convenient target. If that is done each time anger starts, a more balanced perspective will be achieved.

Angry people tend to jump to — and act on — conclusions, and some of those conclusions can be very inaccurate. The first reaction to a heated discussion should be to slow down and think through the response. Don't say the first thing that comes into mind, but slow down and think carefully about what should be said next. At the same time, listen carefully to what the other person is saying and take time before answering.

Some psychologists recommend using humor which can help defuse rage in a number of ways. On the football field, that is a very risky proposition. The humor may make the official appear flippant and make the situation worse.

The following are some questions you can ask yourself when you notice you are getting angry.

WHERE IS THE EVIDENCE?

Is there sufficient evidence to back up the interpretation you have made of the event that is causing the anger? For example, a defensive player is knocked down at the point of attack and the coach claims you missed a takedown hold. The official's first thought is, "He didn't see that; he made that up." Is there a chance that really happened?

IS THERE ANOTHER WAY OF LOOKING AT THE EVENT?

Try to entertain one or two other explanations for what you've interpreted as "deliberate provocation." Often that is enough to at least decrease anger to the level of mild frustration. Using the scenario from the above point, you might ask yourself if you really saw the whole play. Were you partially blocked out? Could it have appeared to be a takedown from his angle?

Rarely are things as catastrophic in reality as they seem in the heat of the moment. The coach said you missed it. So what? Will it amount to anything by the end of the game? Will he forget about it two plays later?

WHAT WILL THE OUTCOME BE?

Thinking of potential outcomes of our actions is not easy, much less when you are in a state of anger. Anger is by nature "single minded." Extreme anger almost always has negative outcomes when it is taken out on another person. Try to train yourself to step into the future in the heat of the moment. What if you do verbally assault the coach? Could it make the game worse?

WHERE IS THE OTHER PERSON COMING FROM?

Anger creates cognitive myopia. Symptomatic of anger is a narrowing of focus on what we perceive as injustice. So it's harder to empathize with others when we are angry. Force yourself to empathize early on, before anger is out of control. Imagine yourself in the other person's shoes. Even just momentarily considering the validity of the other person's feelings can be enough to ebb anger to the extent that it is manageable.

Anger is one of the most difficult emotions to control, because it has a sudden onset and escalates quickly. The key to effectively controlling anger is to slow things down. Once the early arousal signs are recognized and you learn to step back and evaluate the situation thoroughly, anger will lose a great deal of its power.

Remember, anger can't be eliminated — and it wouldn't be a good idea if it were. In spite of all efforts, things will happen that will cause anger; and sometimes it will be justifiable anger. Games will be filled with frustration, pain, loss and the unpredictable actions of others. That can't be changed; but the way such events affect an official can be changed. Controlling angry responses can keep them from making creating more unhappiness in the long run.

CHAPTER

07

ADD IT UP: USE MATH SKILLS TO MANAGE THE GAME

A football official must be a mathematician of sorts because football is a game of numbers. The players are numbered, the yardlines are numbered, etc. From the perspectives of the coaches and players, there are even more numbers: the plays, the holes to run through and so on. Fortunately, officials need not be overly concerned with those. Knowledge of calculus or algebra is not necessary, but mental arithmetic computed quickly is often necessary. Officials must have a rudimentary understanding of arithmetic to properly officiate a football game.

COUNTING

Officials have several counting responsibilities. The players of both teams must be counted before every down. A currently popular system of signaling the count features a fist held up by cooperating officials before the snap: in a five-man crew, the referee with the umpire, and the wings with the back judge. Because teams usually shuffle players in and out during certain situations, it is especially critical to count players before kick plays and after a change of possession. The referee and umpire count the offense, while there is some variety in which officials count the defense. Clearly, the back judge (crew of five) is the primary counter of the defense and he may be assisted by one or both wings. On some crews, both wings count the defense, while on others, the wings count the team whose sideline they are on. That results in three officials counting the offense and two counting the defense.

Under NFHS rules, in order for team A's formation to be legal, there must be seven players on the line. (In NCAA, it is illegal to have more than four players in the backfield.) In most cases, it's easier to check to see that no more than four players are in the backfield. If the offense has only 10 players, only three may be in the backfield to meet the seven-men-on-the-line requirement. Wing officials should look for the referee's signal regarding his count; if he signals fewer than 11 on the field but there are four in the backfield, you know there's a problem. If he signals 11 and there are four in the backfield, you don't need to count the linemen.

Counting four downs is very simple arithmetically, but sometimes confusion leads to mishaps. First of all, the linesman should check the down box regularly. Periodically an entire half goes by without a linesman ever looking back to verify the number on the down box. Sometimes an official loses track of a down and has to rely on a crewmate to get back on track. Fortunately, with all five officials tracking each down, an error should be rare.

Giving a team an extra down, as opposed to shorting a team a down, is the more common of the two errors. It usually happens when penalties occur and officials aren't paying attention and affirming whether a down is lost or replayed. In addition to holding up fingers, calling out the downs to one another is a form of insurance that officials know the proper down during any point in a game.

The box holder is sometimes one of the culprits in a down error. He may fail to flip the box when a penalty is declined. In addition to the linesman, the line judge should be checking the box on every play. Perhaps the greatest opportunity for a down error occurs when a penalty that includes loss of down is enforced and the crew neglects to count it. Also, a team may be shorted by enforcing a loss of down with a penalty that does not have that provision, such as an ineligible receiver downfield.

PENALTY ENFORCEMENT

The vast majority of distance penalties are either five, 10 or 15 yards. For most penalties, the math is very simple, but there are two challenges: crossing the 50 yardline and half-the-distance enforcement.

Play: Second and 10 on team B's 44 yardline. During A2's short run beyond the line, A6 is flagged for clipping at team B's 47 yardline. The penalty is accepted. **Ruling:** In NFHS play, the penalty is enforced from the spot of the foul, team B's 47 yardline. That means three yards to midfield, then 12 yards to team A's 38 yardline, where it will be second and 28. In NCAA, the foul is enforced from the previous spot, team B's 44 yardline. That means six yards to midfield, then nine yards to team A's 41 yardline, where it will be second and 25.

When crossing the 50 yardline, do the math as explained above. First, calculate the yards to midfield, subtract that from the amount of the penalty, then subtract that remaining amount from 50.

The most difficult aspect of half-the-distance enforcement is probably recognizing when it applies. Under NCAA rules, half-the-distance enforcement does not apply for defensive pass interference unless the previous spot was on or inside team B's two yardline or a try was attempted from on or inside team B's three yardline. More than one umpire in NFHS games has walked defensive pass interference from team B's 25 yardline to the 10 yardline. Actually, the calculation is pretty fundamental. In the preceding scenario, half of 25 is 12-1/2, and that is where the ball is placed.

The key yardlines are the 30, 20 and 10. Inside the 30 yardline, all 15-yard penalties are half-the-distance; at the 20 yardline, 15- and 10-yard penalties are half-the-distance; at or inside the 10 yardline, all penalties are half-the-distance.

THE CLOCK

The play clock is a factor on every play. NFHS allows states to decide if they may use a visible play clock.

It's a good idea for the back judge (crew of five) or the referee (crews of less than five) to know when the play count will expire. That means the responsible official should make it a habit to look at the clock or his watch with the ready signal. In fact, each crew should have a designated clock-watcher who checks to see the clock is stopped for plays out of bounds, incomplete passes, fumble recoveries, scores, etc. In crews of five, the back judge counts off the last five seconds by using a visible counting signal. With fewer than five, the referee can verbalize that team A has five seconds remaining.

At critical moments in games, it is also important for someone to watch how a clock is started after it's been stopped. Unethical (or oblivious) clock operators have been known to start the clock early if the visiting team is driving for a crucial score, or delay the clock at the start of a play when the home team is in a hurry-up offense. Occasionally a crew will discover quite late that a play taking seven or nine seconds shows a clock lapse of only a few seconds, or that several additional seconds have come off the clock when they shouldn't have.

Having officials checking the clock at critical junctures alerts the officials to a probable delay foul. If team A doesn't break the huddle with at least 10 seconds remaining, it is going to be difficult to snap the ball before the play clock reaches zero.

CHAPTER

IT'S STILL A
JUNGLE OUT THERE

The six-page feature, titled "A War on Ferocity," appeared as the cover story in a well-known weekly sports publication. An explanatory paragraph above the main text (known in publishing parlance as a deck) noted that NFL officials are "tightening up on rules and carefully studying game films for hidden infractions."

A rash of serious injuries to marquee players was blamed on late hits, unnecessary roughness, forearm shivers, clothesline tackles and kicks to the ribs of downed opponents. The story cited incidents in which a defenseless quarterback was punched by a defensive back brazen enough to do it in full view of officials. The transgressor was promptly and properly penalized and ejected. Several incidents of defenders twisting the limbs of defenseless running backs in an effort to "soften them up" were also reported.

To counter those and other acts of brutality, the article noted that officials were blowing their whistles sooner when a play ended to encourage players to stop the mayhem before it got out of hand.

But not everybody interviewed for the story thought the game was morphing into something more closely resembling pro wrestling. Said the kicker for the Dallas Cowboys, "The players today are better rounded and more intelligent. The game's more technical. There's more polish. That just doesn't leave any place for stupid, dirty football. Why, I think we could cut off the officials and play without them."

Ready for a surprise? The story quoted appeared in an issue dated Nov. 11, 1963. (Oddly, the cover photo is of a referee signaling holding rather than personal foul, but that's neither here or there.) For non-history buffs and those of you too young to remember, the issue hit the newsstands 11 days before a different type of savagery was perpetrated, allegedly from the sixth floor of the Texas School Book Depository in Dallas.

The point here is that rough play is nothing new. According to the NCAA website, college presidents beseeched President Teddy Roosevelt in 1905 to ban the game from campuses. The college leaders pointed to 18 onfield deaths that season alone. Roosevelt reacted by conducting a summit involving representatives of Harvard, Yale and Princeton, the most influential football-playing schools at that time. The roughest of the Roughriders convinced them that either the rules had to be changed to eliminate the foul play and brutality, or the game would be outlawed.

Roosevelt and his contemporaries would probably be shocked to see how the game they saved has evolved. Bigger, stronger and faster athletes are wearing equipment that would amaze turn-of-the-last-century types. In fact, some of that gear and some of the fouls that occurred in those bygone days weren't around even in 1963.

For instance, helmets were not mandatory until 1943. Facemasks were not required prior to 1954. In '63, grabbing the facemask of an opponent was illegal unless the opponent involved was the runner. The guy with the ball was essentially fair game.

"We were looking at some films one day, and we saw a couple of plays where the runner almost had his ripped off by a facemask tackle," said the late Pete Rozelle, then-commissioner of the NFL. "We decided we better make it illegal."

Here's an example from the other side of the coin: Running into the kicker was deemed so heinous that it carried a five-yard penalty and an automatic first down. It was several years before the rules were changed such that only the yardage portion of the penalty was enforced.

Today's rulebooks do a good job of identifying dangerous fouls that are subject to penalty. Blocks such as clipping, blocking in the back and chop blocks are almost universally illegal. In NFHS play, blocking below the waist can only occur during a brief, specific period of time just after the ball is snapped. The same is true with blocking below the waist in NCAA games.

Among the other acts forbidden by the NFHS are fighting, kicking, late hits, throwing a helmet, spearing, butt blocking and slapping an opponent's head. Punching or kicking an opponent is considered fighting regardless if the blow finds its mark. Roughing the passer, kicker, holder and snapper are illegal under specific circumstances.

NCAA rules are virtually identical with some additions, including but not limited to continuously contacting an opponent's helmet (including the facemask) and leaping (running forward in an attempt to block a scoring kick and landing on an opponent).

A foul that officials need to call more often is contact with a player who is obviously out of the play. Perhaps the most common examples are charging into an opponent standing near a pile after a fumble, smacking an opponent on the side of the field opposite of the one on which the play has been run and drilling a receiver after a pass has fallen short or gone over the receiver's head. Those situations involve defenseless players. It's up to the officials to protect them.

One of the roadblocks to preventing late hits is the old coaching adage, "Play until the whistle blows." Officials know that the whistle doesn't kill the ball; the whistle only confirms the ball is dead. If the ball is not visible, officials are trained to withhold the whistle. It's a situation in which coaching philosophy conflicts with officiating beliefs. Because the mechanics are not likely to change, it is incumbent on coaches to ditch that ages-old principle. Sadly, that's not likely to happen anytime soon.

There's a reason rough play is almost an annual point of emphasis in both rulebooks. When you think that the concerns go back to early 1900s, it indicates the problem isn't going away. Will those who follow us long after we're gone look back on the 2010s and shake their heads, wondering why the problem wasn't addressed in our time, or will they look upon this as the generation that made the problem go away? It's a question only we can answer.

CHAPTER

09

FIVE WAYS TO
MESS UP A GAME

As any veteran official can readily attest, there are lots of ways to screw up a football game. But in the grand hit parade of football officiating screw-ups, there are five errors in particular a crew can commit from which it will be difficult, if not impossible, to recover. See how many are on your list as well.

1. BLOW A RULE

That may seem self-evident, but it constantly bears repeating. If a crew erroneously applies a rule (especially if the mistake has a bearing on the outcome of the game), the crew may find itself in hip-high quicksand for a long time to come. Indeed, careers have been lost because of that.

One mistake that often gets made is that the rest of the crew relies on the referee to properly enforce penalties. The umpire does the walking, but he gets his marching orders from the referee. If neither of them called the foul, however, what can happen is that the calling official reports the foul, then turns away and tunes out, as does the rest of the crew. That is why we have a checks-and-balances system.

The line judge, umpire and head linesman must be certain they know what the foul was, from where it should be enforced and how much yardage should be assessed. When the umpire gets to the correct starting point, the head linesman should also be at that point and both should walk off the yardage independently of each other. The line judge should already be at the succeeding spot. If the umpire stops and the line judge is at that spot and the head linesman ends up there, they can be pretty certain that the correct yardage was marked off and from the right spot.

But maybe it wasn't. Maybe they thought the foul was defensive pass interference (15 yards from the previous spot) when it was actually defensive holding (10 yards). In those cases, having the umpire, head linesman and line judge end up in the same spot means nothing, because all three are wrong. To prevent that, it is imperative that the calling official pay careful attention to how the penalty is being administered, so that he can jump in if something seems amiss.

Even if you're a rookie and/or the only person on the crew who thinks the crew is about to screw up, step in and make your voice heard. If you're right, you can save the entire crew and if you're wrong, so what? Almost all referees will appreciate that and as for the handful who don't, don't worry about them. If a rules error occurs in a game, it is ultimately the fault of every person on that crew.

2. EMPLOY POOR VERBAL AND NONVERBAL COMMUNICATION SKILLS

If coaches get the idea you're unapproachable, if you come across as overbearing, if you throw your flag in such a way that it looks like you're glad to have nailed the offender, you're fighting a losing battle from then on.

The communication effort must start from the time you arrive at the game site. Be polite to the school people you encounter; don't act like some big shot who expects everyone to bend over backward to accommodate you.

Be professional when you visit with the coaches before the game. Don't take a cookie-cutter approach and treat all coaches the same way. Some want to talk but some just want you to take care of business and get out of there. If you prattle on endlessly, you'll turn them off. Don't make borderline jokes because, despite what you assume, your audience may not appreciate that brand of humor. And don't make throwaway comments that can come back to haunt you. A few years ago a veteran umpire told one of the coaches, who was 0-4 at that time, "No matter how the score ends up, we know it will be a tough game." As innocent as that sounds, the coach took it to mean that it was assumed he was going to lose and he threw that in the officials' faces when a call went against him in the game.

During the game, ignore the static from the sidelines when you can. But when you've had enough, especially from an assistant coach, don't go on the attack. Just say, "Coach, I've heard enough. It's time to turn the page." Or say to the head coach, "I need you to get your assistant calmed down." Stay away from threats. If it continues and you have no choice but to call an unsportsmanlike conduct foul, don't launch the flag to the moon; just toss it toward the field.

Get the number of the fouling players to the coaches. If you don't know it at the time, tell them you'll get it when you can and let them know. If they ask for explanations, provide them when you can do so without interfering with your own duties. Treat the players with respect; don't call them "son" or the like.

3. MISS A DOWN

Just because he has the down box at his disposal and all those assistants known as the chain crew, don't rely entirely on the head linesman for the down and distance in every situation. Sure, he is primarily responsible for that, but stuff happens.

The referee should always make sure to communicate with the head linesman the same way. After a play ends and dead-ball officiating duties are taken care of, the referee should signal the next down to the linesman, who returns the signal and then tells the box man to flip to the next down. Same routine every play. Between downs other members of the crew have a signaling routine with each other. Don't just go through the motions. If someone is not on the same page, stop the game and confer. Don't sit back and assume that because you've got second down and everyone else has third, you're wrong. Maybe there was a dead-ball foul that led to confusion for your crewmates.

Colorado got a fifth down in its game with Missouri in 1990. A penalty was involved and confusion reigned. It's 20 years later and that topic still comes up. The officials involved never lived it down.

4. BE A NITPICKER

A real good way to irretrievably screw up a game is to call things in a hyper-technical manner from the start. No one, least of all the coaches, players and spectators, wants a flag day. Technically, there is a foul on virtually every play, but we'll rightfully be accused of taking the game away from the kids if we call everything. Err on the side of not calling non-safety-related fouls but calling the safety-related ones. And in line with that, don't keep two flags and don't let the one you have hang way out of your pocket. That makes it look like you just can't wait to start throwing. If you have two fouls on a play, throw your hat for the second one.

If the middle linemen aren't breaking the line of the snapper's waist, warn them if it's borderline, then call it and ring them right up if it's flagrant. If you warn, let the coach know you did.

Call a lot of ticky-tack fouls and you'll destroy the game and, moreover, develop a reputation in your area that is not conducive to good schedules or to advancement.

5. DON'T BE A GOOD DEAD-BALL OFFICIAL

Football, as we all know, is an intense, physical game. Players are coached for months to pound the stuffing out of the other guy and to play on the edge. If we turn too quickly to get a new ball from a ballboy in the side zone, thus missing an off-the-ball whack to the head 10 yards in front of us, disaster can ensue. Indeed, an argument can be made that of all the things that can cause a crew to lose control of a game to the point of no return, poor dead-ball officiating is the prime culprit.

We can't afford to take our eyes off the players too quickly, or fail to use the "halo" concept: That involves the notion that the covering official watches the immediate area around where the runner is tackled, the next-nearest officials watch the larger halo around them (15-20 yards) and the other officials watch the rest of the field. If we do that, we're much more likely to see the guy knock the other guy into the next century 25 yards away from the ball.

That is where umpires, in particular, come in. Much of the testiness that can happen in a game occurs because of things taking place at the line of scrimmage. A good umpire will sense that something is brewing and that he needs to become a cop. An umpire cannot just look for holding and spot the ball after plays end; he must pay attention to what everyone in his proximity is doing and saying and how he can defuse problems that he sees developing.

When officials don't do a good job of dead-ball officiating, wars can break out. Just let that happen and see what becomes of the rest of the game and your reputation as a crew.

CHAPTER 10

THE JOB DOESN'T END WHEN THE BALL IS DEAD

An official covering the play watches a runner cross the sideline, gets to the spot, kills the clock and plants his foot. Then he looks down to make sure his foot is secure on the correct place.

That is a sin. At least, it's a violation of the 10th Officiating Commandment as written by former NFL Director of Officiating Jerry Seeman. His commandment was, "Thou shalt be a great dead-ball official."

Well, perhaps calling it a sin is a little severe. Let's back off and call it a mistake. Some college officials delight in coming to local association meetings and scolding fellow officials who stare at the ground when establishing a spot. "The ground will never commit a foul," they say.

The point they're trying to make, however, is a valid one. Once you've determined what the dead-ball place is, if you keep staring at it, you'll be ignoring all the players in the game. Any action an official can take to keep his attention fixed on players when a bunch of them move beyond the sideline will be a sound practice. Yet many officials cannot break the eyes-on-the-ground habit.

Former NFL line judge Bama Glass once told a colleague that the first habit he had to break when advancing to the pros was running down the sideline and planting a foot, turning to the field and serenely killing the clock.

"That may be three, four seconds of elapsed time," Glass said. "It's unacceptable. The clock's gotta be killed the instant a play carries outside the field of play. It's one signal you use while on the run."

The NFL has established efficient and effective techniques for getting an accurate spot while watching players who are out of bounds. Covering officials hop around obstacles if necessary, all the while focusing entirely on players. It is difficult to understand why the efficient and effective techniques of the NFL are not adopted wholesale across the nation. Surely, officials see them displayed weekly, for half a year. Moreover, their basic pragmatism is easy to accept. Officials should also be watching receivers and defenders — not the ball — after an incomplete pass. Watch peripheral players after fumble recoveries too, after any kind of runback. Someone could be upset and may drive into an opponent unnecessarily. Alertness is not exclusively a dead-ball proposition. Sensible seeing-eye behaviors during live action may be categorized under several principles, one of which can be called "dropping keys." The respective officials should observe what their keys do following a snap and how eyes should shift — many times in milliseconds — as a play unfolds. Here's a single for-instance. An umpire in a high school game may be watching a guard and snapper when a play starts, but if the snapper is buffeted by a noseguard and the guard next to him pulls, the umpire must redirect his focus instantly toward the tackle in the direction of the pulling guard. That is because the tackle's block will likely be the essential block on the play. Oh, other blocks will be important too, but those can be observed by other officials. Those officials should also be abandoning their initial keys once a runner moves beyond the free-blocking zone.

So here's principle number one: Know when to drop your key and observe with precision the subsequent phase of a play.

Next, let's address the "Magnetic Corollary." When the ball moves toward or along a sideline, either in possession of a runner — sweep, pass reception, interception, kick runback or loose ball after possession — all 22 players will be drawn to the ball like iron filings pulled to a magnet. Such mass action leaves many players vulnerable, with backs toward opponents, tempting them to hit from behind. In truth a secondary "subset" principle can be applied: When the ball is outside the hash, interior officials (referee, umpire and back judge) have no business watching it. They should be looking at players who do not have the ball, blockers and potential tacklers, while adopting an "inside-out" perspective.

That principle can't be an absolute, though; it's more of an "in general" attitude, because there are times when interior officials should indeed follow a ball or a runner into a side zone. A passer flushed and fleeing, a fumble propelled toward the sideline are just two occurrences.

Those are useful topics to be explored in crew conferences, to define coverage responsibilities under varying live-ball circumstances.

Another principle is, beware of "curling" propensities. Curling can take place on sideline plays. Players begin by moving upfield or downfield and then bend toward the side zone when action calls them there, as already described.

But there are two other instances of potential curling that deserve mention. One is lead blockers on a sweep. Sometimes blockers get too far out ahead of a runner and bypass assigned blocking targets. In such cases — rare, but they do occur — blockers may be in position to hit pursuers from behind. That is where umpire and wing officials can demonstrate identical focus. An alert back judge can contribute another pair of sharp eyes in those instances too.

The curl can be devastating though and can lead to "negative clustering." It can happen when wing officials hurry toward the pile on every play inside the hash. That technique can result in a "bucket brigade." One official picks up the ball and hands it to another official who turns and gives it to a third for placement. What that does is to narrow the focus of officials, and it causes officials to ignore players behind them.

If a wideout and a cornerback engage in a tussle after a play, a wing official may not observe that if he's squeezing in excessively. Sometimes the referee also rushes to the dead-ball spot after a draw play. When a passer drops into a pocket, rushers are often driven around behind him. In the instance described one defender who had curled past the quarterback returned and drove a shoulder solidly into the quarterback's kidneys, propelling him face forward with a vicious hit. That's one that's got to be caught.

Clearly, clustering can be a detrimental mechanic. It opens up places on the field where no watchful officiating eye can observe and respond properly.

CHAPTER

THE EFFECTIVE
CREW CHIEF

Not every official is cut out to be a crew chief. A crew chief must have a number of attributes, and have superior skills in those areas. By the same token, the best crew chiefs are able to delegate and assign tasks to the other members of their crew so that the rest of the crew feels a sense of ownership and accountability.

The referee is the face of the crew. He more than anyone represents the conference or league that assigned the crew. A referee who acts, looks and performs like a professional reflects positively on the conference.

What traits does the NFL look for when seeking its next crew chiefs? Is there a personality type or skill set those elite candidates need to have?

"It's got to be someone who is respected by his fellow officials and will be respected by his crew," said Mike Pereira, former NFL vice president of officiating. "There's the dynamic of the referee knowing how to get the best out of his crew.

"As a side judge or a line judge, 80 percent of your value is based on what you actually call and 20 percent is that other area that involves professionalism and decisiveness," Pereira added. "When you become a referee, I think it flips. Eighty percent of your value comes from what you do off the field, not what you do on the field. So it's got to be someone who understands that. You need someone who knows in that role he's got to be a teacher, a motivator and a caretaker. He's got to help guys when they're down and control guys when they are up. He's got to continue to teach all year. He's almost got to give up himself a little bit and recognize that it's not about him, it's more about the crew. It takes a special form of leadership to accomplish that."

Although not all referees are former athletes, they can raise the level of the crew by thinking of each game as a competition. Each crew wants to be the best; the referee can foster that desire by challenging the crew to "win" each game.

Perhaps more than anything else, the crew chief is a manager. He must take charge and direct the activities of the crew throughout each game and throughout each season.

That management must be balanced with the necessity of avoiding the "god complex" in which the referee feels the need to take care of every miniscule detail. A successful crew chief delegates responsibility to crew members. Not only does that take pressure off the referee to do everything, it ensures that each member feels like a part of the crew.

"The referee has to set some parameters on issues such as when we're going to watch film and when we're going to do the pregame," said Steve Shaw, a former Southeastern Conference (SEC) referee and now SEC coordinator of football officials. "But the rest is delegator. Even though you're the referee, there are bright people on the crew and a lot of people capable of a lot of different things. Over the years I (became) more delegator than dictator because I think you get more done as a delegator."

When the referee has less experience than another member on the crew, the referee can solicit ideas from the veteran. But suggestions from other crew members should be given equal consideration.

It is essential that the crew chief get a handle on the personalities of the crew. Officials are usually aggressive people with healthy egos, yet they are people with vastly different temperaments, personalities and quirks. The crew chief's job is to figure out what makes each of his crewmates tick.

If one crew member is a nervous or exceptionally serious individual, the crew chief may joke around with him to loosen him up. Many crews have at least one member who is extremely hard on himself when it comes to self-judging his performance. Such a member may benefit from praise or extra tutoring. If a member is chronically late, the crew chief must impress upon that member that his tardiness is affecting the crew in a negative way.

"I am a big believer in the power of positive criticism, that people learn through praise," said veteran NFL referee Ed Hochuli. "If the line judge is making a mistake consistently but the head linesman does it right, I would much rather praise the head linesman for what he did as the example to the line judge of how he should have been doing it, rather than criticize the line judge for not doing it.

"Now, depending on how unreceptive the line judge is, or if you think he's not picking it up, then you hint a little bit more," Hochuli added. "I haven't said, 'You screwed up and didn't do it.' That doesn't mean you don't criticize. But you should try to make the tone as positive as possible."

Pac-12 referee Jack Folliard takes a similar approach with his crew. "I like to teach with leadership and by example, but I also inject a lot of humor into teaching," he says. "Officials at the major college level have the talent, skills and rules knowledge. But a lot of times they need help with the mental side of things. It's a very stressful atmosphere. When officials make mistakes, they know it. The last thing you want to do is get down on them. We do a lot of kidding on our crew. We keep people honest. We use what I call serious humor. I emphasize that it's a serious avocation that needs to be fun. If you can't create a fun teaching atmosphere, it's not going to work."

It's a good idea to keep track of what is going on in the everyday lives of the crew members. Has there been a death in the family? Has someone lost a job? The entire crew needs to know that, which requires keeping in touch with crewmates in the offseason as well as during the season.

The crew chief must foster an environment in which the crew can engage in honest and open communication. If a crew member feels his opinion will be dismissed out of hand, a wall forms. Seeing that may prevent other members from providing valuable input.

"A lot of officials are afraid to talk to a fellow official, particularly their crew chief, because they think it's going to get back to the supervisor," Folliard said. "My crew knows that absolutely does not happen. They know if they take me into confidence, they have my word it stays with me." "You have got to be able to project yourself in a positive way," Pereira says. "A referee can carry a crew or he can destroy a crew. If a coach is confident in a referee but the crew is struggling, he'll still have confidence in the crew because of the weight the referee carries."

Referees must realize they are not above constructive criticism from the crew. The crew chief must hold himself to the same level of accountability as every other official. Mistakes should be addressed and attempts to correct them made. If a crew member is struggling, the referee must recognize that and take the lead in offering advice on how the official can improve.

"My crew doesn't hesitate to take me aside and say, 'You're not doing this right,'" Folliard said.

The bottom line is that a crew takes on the personality of the referee. A crew chief who is calm, confident and open is likely to pass on those traits to the other officials, while one who is up tight, closed-minded or dictatorial will be resented, or worse, not trusted.

CHAPTER

WHAT IT TAKES TO BE A RESPECTED OFFICIAL

All officials, by nature of their position, garner respect to varying degrees simply by walking onto the field. Coaches and players are exposed to officials for relatively short periods and in limited circumstances. To gain the respect of peers, though, an official must earn it. Here are suggestions to improve your reputation.

Support your partners. The only true friends an official has on the field are crewmates. That trust cannot be violated. Learn a lesson from a high school baseball umpire who got embroiled in a dispute over whether an infield line drive was short-hopped or not. An undeserved double play was at stake and the original ruling was reversed. The umpire made the mistake of openly blaming his partner for not making the original call (not true). He has yet to live that down and many umpires do not want to work with him because they simply don't trust him.

Control your ego. All officials have an ego. A strong ego is necessary to survive as an official, but there are excesses. An official is better than he gets credit for, but still not as good as he thinks he is. Avoid publicity. Unless the local paper wants to do a human interest story, any attention given an official is bound to have negative consequences. Controversy is newsworthy. Making the right call game after game, season after season, is not.

Officials who are money-hungry or out for personal gain can be readily identified by fellow officials. Officials are smart enough to know when they are being used as a stepping stone.

BE HONEST

There is no excuse for lying. When you make a mistake, admit it. If you're not sure what you saw, say so. Everyone has made more than one call they wish they could have back. Learn from those errors and strive not to repeat them.

RESPECT OTHERS

Coaches and players deserve respect. Officials may not agree with the plays called. In a playoff game, a coach leading by seven points with five minutes remaining in the game called for a fake punt on fourth and two from deep in his own territory. His player was stopped short of the line-to-gain and the opponents easily scored a touchdown soon thereafter. The coach survived his gaffe when the opponent's try failed.

KEEP A POSITIVE VIEW

A negative attitude and constant complaining do not inspire others. An official was once cautioned about scolding players who fouled and told "coaches don't like it." His reply, "All coaches are (rectal openings)." Officials cannot carry prejudice and that gentleman soon thereafter lost interest in officiating.

GET IT RIGHT

It's great to look good and come up with the right call. Decisiveness — the quick and correct call — is a wonderful attribute. It's better to look clumsy and get it right than to look sharp and get it wrong. You can sell a bad call until the film is reviewed. The highest levels of college football have incorporated instant replay as an officiating tool. Lower-division college and high school officials cannot use replay or other TV equipment to make any decisions, but anything else is fair game. Sometimes getting it right takes time.

BE PERSONABLE

Officials miss out when they avoid being personable. There is a fine line between being personable and being chummy, but there are a few things you can do to make yourself come across as warmer than a robot.

Some referees make a point of finding the quarterback's name in every game he worked. They say it quickly establishes a rapport. To be sure, the referee is likely to have the most contact with quarterbacks. Make him your man in terms of contact. Chances are he'll get the point quickly and be receptive to whatever appeal you bring to him.

Never refer to players as "Boys" because that's patronizing, even racially offensive in some cultures. Also avoid "Kids" and "Son." Referring to individual players by their uniform number seems impersonal, but it is the safest route. "Gentlemen" is best when addressing the entire group. "Sir" or "Coach" is appropriate with coaches.

CHAPTER

THINK BEYOND
THE GRIDIRON

Officials who work a single sport sometimes have a tendency to be a little myopic. If football is their game, they follow football, read about football and learn from football officials. Same thing if it's soccer, basketball, baseball or softball.

Multi-sport officials are often more open to seeing the possibilities offered by studying another sport. They've lived it.

While it's true that a confirmed football-only official will never need to know the rules pertaining to free throws, hit batters or corner kicks, officials in one sport can find common ground with officials who work other sports by taking a peek at what officials in other sports are learning. You don't have to start attending meetings at the local soccer officials association or attend a basketball camp or umpire school to get that info.

For instance, here's some advice that was originally directed at soccer officials: "You may focus on the heat or cold; the crowd and that obnoxious spectator who seems to have your number; the coach who is subtly gaming you. You can overhear and be drawn into the conversations off the bench and coach, particularly during lulls in the game." Who among us hasn't had that problem? The solution, according to the author, is to "try to see if you can 'go into the bubble' and tune them out by positively focusing on your cues in the game."

A question often asked by officials — particularly those striving for postseason assignments or to move up a level — is, "What do supervisors want?" Kathy Strahm, formerly the head of the NCAA Softball Umpire Improvement Program, was once asked what umpires can do to improve.

"Model yourselves on the best umpires in the game," Strahm said. "Find that umpire who is the best game manager and copy her methods. Seek out the best plate umpire and determine what makes him so good and copy that. Look for the umpire whose signals are simply art in motion."

Sounds like the makings of a good football official, too, doesn't it?

Strahm also spoke about the special avocation we enjoy. "Realize that being an umpire is such an honorable profession — it's actually all about honor — and integrity and dignity and respect. How can a new official not be proud and confident when he realizes that?"

It is often assumed that only veterans can dispose great advice. While it is often true that less experienced officials can learn from veterans, the graybeards can also learn from the rookies. Material directed at baseball umpires noted that.

"Old and new alike have something to offer each other if they are willing to keep an open mind, listen, digest and adapt," the writer noted. "The veteran has learned first-hand about common-sense rules enforcement; handling odd situations and coaches and players who get weird; dealing with weather, averting problems ... and finessing assigners."

Good information obtained in camps should be shared. "Younger officials comprise the bulk of the audiences (at camps and clinics), meaning they end up being the vehicles through which new information is imparted to some old ears, if it ever is at all," the column continued. "Virtually the only way for old dogs to learn those new tricks, which might actually improve our work, is for a pup who attended those camps to tell us what went on there."

Officials in all sports have to deal with unruly fans. A column written for basketball referees offered advice on addressing crowd-related issues.

"The first step in this process is to know who the site manager is," the columnist offered. "Officials should introduce themselves to him/her when they arrive and find out how to contact that worthy individual if needed during the game."

Fans in basketball are, of course, much closer to the action than those in football. Yet in both sports, the following advice makes sense. "Once the game starts, the ... officials would be wise to ignore fan behavior unless it approaches a flagrant level. When fan behavior breaks their concentration on the game action, officials should summon the site manager. Under no circumstances should an official enter into a confrontation with a fan."

Randy Christal is one of the most veteran crew chiefs working football in the Big 12 Conference. He's officiated football since 1970, including the 1996 Rose Bowl the 1997 Sugar Bowl and the 2003 national championship Fiesta Bowl. Additionally, Christal is a longtime college baseball umpire with eight College World Series assignments under his belt. Throw in another 15 years worth of high school and small college basketball and it's safe to say, Christal has a broad range of officiating knowledge to draw from. He shares some of the benefits of working multiple sports.

INCREASED AWARENESS

"I find baseball has helped my football officiating because calling a balk increases my awareness for false starts in football," he says. "The balk can be such a subtle move and as an umpire you must be keenly aware."

PERSONAL SKILLS

"Football has helped my baseball umpiring in dealing with coaches," Christal says. "You don't yell at football coaches; you simply enforce the rules. Baseball is a bit more confrontational, but you still must be the adult — unlike many baseball coaches."

REACTION TIME AND DECISIVENESS

"Timing is the key in all sports: You look, you think and then you make the call," says Christal. "In basketball if you do that too slow, they have scored and are halfway back down the court. It's more of a reaction thing in basketball, but it helps you learn to trust your instincts in other sports."

Five different sports, but information and advice that any official can use. When it comes down to it, we all do pretty much the same thing, have the same goals and share passion for the games we work. All you need is an open mind.

CHAPTER

14

AVOID THE 'CRASH AND BURN'

When speaking of onfield blunders, Bill Carollo, the retired NFL Super Bowl referee who now serves as coordinator of football officials for the Big Ten and other conferences, comes straight to the point. "When you have mistakes," he says, "it always, always, always involves bad communications."

Many officials know the feeling, that errors by you or your crewmates have led to the feeling a game has been akin to a plane crash, but to understand how those things happen, it might be better to examine a plane crash.

Malcolm Gladwell, in his book *Outliers: The Story of Success*, writes that most airplane crashes aren't the result of a single, catastrophic event. His statistics say that often the weather is poor, but not terrible, and the pilot may be somewhat stressed. As a result, he or she might not be thinking as clearly and might be less likely to act decisively. Most of the time, the crew is running late and 52 percent of the time, they have been awake for more than 12 hours. Forty-four percent of the time, they have not worked with each other before. Throw in occasional arrogance or the lack of some vital information the crew needs and the result, claims Gladwell, is apparent: They set themselves up for failure, which often means their own demise.

But let's think about it. Had we not been talking about commercial flight crews, we could have been talking about officiating crews. The failure modes are often the same.

Have you ever had a bad night on the field that started when emotions got too high? You end up having so many fires to fight that you get out of that "zone" you want to be in and start hesitating when you should be acting. How often does the trouble start when someone kicks a call and the crew doesn't get together and fix it, if it can? It doesn't help either to be trying to work a tough game after eight hours in the office and an hour's drive just to get there. What about working with an unfamiliar crew? You know your tendencies, but you might lose a little bit of focus on your own work until you decide to trust your crewmates. And we all know what it's like to work with Joe Infallible or a crewmate who, for whatever reason, seems content to stand back and let you fry instead of stepping up to help. While it's tempting to shrug off some mistakes as the result of unusual or unforeseeable situations, learning from mistakes helps prevent them from biting you again. While having a good pregame is important — especially when you don't know the other officials — a good *post*game is even more valuable.

Preparing for success by reminding yourself of things you've screwed up doesn't sound like the power of positive thinking. Can you imagine Phil Mickelson standing over a downhill, eight-footer, saying to himself, "OK, you missed the last three. Now you're ready to make this one for the tournament"? Well, that is what top officials do. They believe that acknowledging their mistakes and taking something positive away from them in preparing for the next game only makes them stronger.

Officiating is like running a hurdle race: Look back at the last hurdle you just stumbled over and you'll miss the next one, which is the only one that matters. When you blow one, the only thing to do is deal with it and move on. That's just as important for others on your crew. A mistake that some officials make is covering for others when, or if it seems like, they're having a tough day, too. If you start trying to call your position plus someone else's, you end up missing a call right in front of you. If officials are successful at dealing with mistakes and getting past them, everyone benefits.

So, it seems like a lot of issues with errors and how you deal with them come down to ego which, paradoxically, both makes us and breaks us as officials. Gladwell sees it in airline incidents, too, in a light that may help us. He claims that the frequency of commercial crashes has decreased in recent years because airlines have succeeded in overcoming the personalities that compound problems and make them dangerous in the cockpit. In his book, he talks about a hypothetical question once put to a group of pilots and co-pilots during a seminar. Suppose, they are asked, their plane is flying directly toward a nasty thunderstorm that is prudent to avoid: How would they tell the pilot?

The researchers, Ute Fischer and Judith Orasanu, found that the wording varied. Some would say, "Turn right, 30 degrees." Plain and simple, right? Others would say, "That return at 25 miles looks mean." A true statement, but what's their point? In between those extremes were shades of gray: "I think we need to deviate right now," to "Let's go around the weather," to "Which direction would you like to deviate?" to "I think it would be wise to turn left or right." OK, we're talking about flying big, expensive aircraft with hundreds of people aboard, in a potentially dangerous situation and the two people who can avert disaster are mincing words. Each of those six sentences leaves more to the interpretation of the listener than the one before it. If you're wide awake and sharp, arguably any of the six should be taken as a requirement to change course. If you're not as sharp, or distracted, or not looking at the radar, most of the same statements might leave room for misinterpretation — or worse, be ignored. Only, "turn right ..." is bound to produce a response, which is the beginning of solving a problem.

Fischer and Orasanu found that the captains overwhelmingly favored the command, "Turn right, 30 degrees," since they were in command; what they say goes. The first officers, instead, went for the most mitigated statement, "That return at 25 miles looks mean," because they weren't the boss. Using mitigated speech is the practice of watering down your message in deference to the sociological factors involved. You choose your words based on how you perceive your status within the group.

It is crucial for everyone to be absolutely truthful about whether they're sure of a call they made and to be able to offer any pertinent information they might have toward resolution of the issue. "I'm not sure," doesn't mean, "I don't know." If officials offer up whatever they observed, whether they know if it's relevant or not, the crew can knit together a competent ruling. You don't want to be sitting in the dressing room after the game and then have someone say, "You know, I'm not sure we got that one right."

While the approaches to the issue may vary, the central point is that effective crews find a way to make effective communication work for them. They work quickly when possible, but deliberately when necessary. They establish a system of checks and balances so that the crew gets a chance to weigh in on difficult rulings through open and frank discussion. And no matter how badly they screw up a call, they own up to it, decide what's best to do next and move on.

Crash and burn ... it never has to happen.